MW00964233

SAVOUR PRESS'S
ILLUSTRATED
all time best
the pasta cookbook
Simple and Delicious Recipes

THE PASTA COOKBOOK

EASY AND DELICIOUS PASTA RECIPES

By
Savour Press

Published by
Savour Press, a DBA of Wentworth Publishing House

Let’s get it started!

Welcome to Savour. Just like anybody, we always feel happy when we get invited to a party, reunions and milestones of our friends and loved ones because of the myriads of menus that we will partake of. When we get home, we want to try out the food that we have tasted and our curiosity sometimes becomes frustrating because we have not followed closely the tip we received from our gracious host. We at Savour want to remove your doubts and frustrations by sharing with you our mouthwatering recipes in every edition of our cookbook. In this edition, we will teach you how to prepare 30 highest rated and popular pasta recipes that will open up your mind about the truth that pasta recipes are very easy to prepare and we want you to try them out once you have read everything in this book. We want you to enjoy every minute of your reading, and eventually, cooking our pasta recipes.

About This Book

We always believe in the saying that if others can do it, why can't I. This is where savor comes in. At Savour, we believe that the art of cooking is an art that needs to be enjoyed by everyone who wants to try out different methods of cooking. In this cookbook, our dear readers will be able to gain insights on how to prepare different pasta recipes that come in a variety of flavors, taste, texture and methods. Our collection of 30 pasta recipes has a short list of ingredients and the cooking direction will not eat much of your time. In most recipes, it starts with cooking the pasta and drain and stir-fry or sauté the sausage or meat, spices, herbs, greens and seasonings and then toss with the cooked pasta. That's it, so simple and easy. Come; let's get ready to have a fun time!

VISIT US AT

www.savourypress.com

Also, by the editors at Savour Press's kitchen

The Chili Cookbook

The Quiche Cookbook

Indian Instant Pot Cookbook

The Cajun and Creole Cookbook

The Grill Cookbook

The Burger Book

The Ultimate Appetizers Cookbook

The West African Cookbook

Korean Seoul Cookbook

The Cast Iron Cookbook

The Holiday Cookbook

The Baking Book

The Crepe Cookbook

JOIN THE SAVOUR PRESS'S READERS CLUB AND RECEIVE A FREE COOKBOOK! JUST STAY UNTIL THE END OF THE BOOK AND CLICK ON THE BOOK OR LINK!

Contents

Conclusion pg.68

Introduction

Whether you are an Italian or not, you have eaten pasta in one point in your life, and will always love to eat pasta, right? We want pasta because they are creamy, cheesy and loaded with seasonings and they are versatile in the like that they can be paired with turkey, chicken, sausage, shrimp, mushroom, pork, beef and vegetables. Overall, the taste of pasta is mouthwatering, delicious and simply irresistible. Our collection of 30 pasta recipes is written in such a way that they are easy to understand, even if you have not taken a course in culinary arts. It starts with Bow Ties with Gorgonzola Sauce and ends with Artichoke Chicken Pasta. We did not categorize them as they can be eaten as part of your breakfast, lunch, dinner, or brunch. There are vegetarian recipes that call for shrimp, and some meatless recipes call for sausage instead, which is still a meat in the real sense of the word.

Enjoy!

Bow Ties with Gorgonzola Sauce

Gorgonzola cheese and half-and-half cream are the secret behind this delectable pasta with the combination of crumbled pork sausage. Mixed herbs are added to neutralize the yellow shade of bow ties.

Servings: 8

Ingredients

1 package (16 ounces) **bulk pork sausage**

1 package (16 ounces) **bow tie pasta**

2 tablespoons **all-purpose flour**

1-1/2 cups **half-and-half cream**

2 tablespoons **butter**

3/4 cup crumbled **Gorgonzola cheese**

3/4 teaspoon **salt**

1/2 teaspoon **lemon-pepper seasoning**

4 cups lightly packed fresh **spinach**

3 tablespoons **fresh basil**, minced

DIRECTIONS:

Cook pasta in a saucepan al dente. Place in a colander and drain. Return the pasta to the saucepan.

Cook in a large skillet the sausage on medium heat for four to six minutes until pinkish color is no longer visible, and crumbles. Remove excess oil.

Melt the butter in a small saucepan over moderate heat. Add the flour and stir until smooth.

Slowly whisk in half-and-half cream and bring mixture to a boil.

Stir frequently and cook for one to two minutes more until thickens.

Remove saucepan from heat, stir in the cheese, lemon pepper and salt.

Stir in cheese sauce, spinach and sausage with cooked pasta and toss until well combined. Garnish with basil on top.

Serve!

Nutritional Information: 953 calories; 52.1 g fat (16.9 g saturated fat); 180 mg cholesterol; 1502 mg sodium; 72.4 g carbohydrate; 0.9 g dietary fiber; 0.1 g total sugars; 47 g protein.

Greek Pasta Toss

If your religious beliefs prevent you from eating pork, but you like pasta with sausage, this recipe is the one for you. It calls for turkey sausage instead of pork. After cooking the spiral pasta, all ingredients are cooked and combined. That's it; your pasta is ready for dinner.

Servings: 4

Ingredients

3/4 pound **Italian turkey sausage links**

3 cups uncooked **whole wheat spiral pasta**

2 minced **garlic cloves**

4 ounces fresh **baby spinach**

1/2 cup pitted **Greek olives**, cut into half

1/4 cup crumbled **feta cheese**

1/3 cup julienned oil-packed **sun-dried tomatoes**

Lemon wedges (optional)

Directions

Remove casings of sausage, set aside. Drain and chop tomatoes and set aside.

Cook pasta in a six-quart stockpot and cook according to what is directed in the package.

Drain the pasta and return to the stockpot.

Cook sausage in a large skillet and crumble on moderate-high heat until it is no longer pink for four to six minutes.

Sauté the garlic for one minute and add to the cooked pasta. Stir in the spinach, tomatoes and olive until the leaves of spinach are wilted. Add the cheese and serve pasta with lemon wedges.

Enjoy!

Nutritional Information: 335 calories; 35 mg cholesterol; 13 g fat (3 g saturated fat); 36 g carbohydrate; 742 mg sodium; 1 g total sugars; 6 g dietary fiber; 19 g protein.

White Cheddar Mac & Cheese

Mac and cheese is an all-time favorite, but with this unique version, you can't live without this pasta in your life. It has the creamy and cheesy goodness with peppery flavor to perk up your day.

Servings: 8

Ingredients

1 package (16 Oz.) small **pasta shells**

1/2 cup cubed **butter**

1/2 cup **all-purpose flour**

1/2 teaspoon ground **chipotle pepper**

1/2 teaspoon **onion powder**

1/2 teaspoon **pepper**

1/4 teaspoon **salt**

2 cups shredded **Manchego cheese**

4 cups **2% milk**

2 cups shredded sharp **white cheddar cheese**

Note: If Manchego cheese is unavailable, use an additional white cheddar cheese instead.

Directions

Cook pasta in a six-quart stockpot and follow the package directions. Drain in a colander and return to the pot.

Melt butter in a large saucepan on a moderate heat.

Stir in all-purpose flour and seasonings until the mixture is smooth.

Whisk in the milk gradually and boil, stirring often, continue cooking for 6-8 minutes, until the mixture has thickened.

Remove the pot from heat. Gradually stir in cheeses until dissolved.

Add the mixture to the pasta and toss to incorporate.

Enjoy!

Nutritional Information: 650 calories; 101 mg cholesterol; 35 g fat (22 g saturated fat); 55 g carbohydrate; 607 mg sodium; 8 g total sugars; 2 g dietary fiber; 27 g protein.

Spicy Shrimp & Penne Pasta

This peppery pasta offers comfort when you are depressed. It gives you satisfaction with the goodness of hot shrimp cooked with red pepper flakes added to the cooked marinara sauce and penne pasta. For a twist, you can use chicken breast instead of shrimp, if you are allergic to sea foods.

Servings: 6

Ingredients

3 cups uncooked **penne pasta**

1 tablespoon **olive oil**, divided

1 tablespoon **butter**, divided

2 pounds (31-40 per pound) uncooked **shrimp**, divided

1 jar (24 ounces) **marinara sauce**

1/2 teaspoon crushed **red pepper flakes**, divided

3/4 cup **half-and-half cream**

4 cups chopped fresh **spinach**

Directions

Peel and devein uncooked shrimp, set aside.

Cook pasta in a six-quart stockpot according to what is indicated in the package, drain and put back to the pot.

Heat half of both oil and butter in a large skillet over moderate high heat.

Sauté half of the shrimp with one-fourth teaspoon pepper flakes for three to five minutes until the shrimp turns pink.

Transfer the cooked shrimp to a mixing bowl. Cook the remaining shrimp.

After the shrimp is cooked, use the same pan and heat the marinara sauce and the cream and slightly boil on moderate heat, stirring to coat.

Stir in spinach until combined and wilted. Add the mixture to the cooked pasta and stir in shrimp. Toss to coat until heated through.

Serve!

Nutritional Information: 395 calories; 12 g fat (4 g saturated fat); 702 mg sodium; 206 mg cholesterol; 38 g carbohydrate; 9 g total sugars; 4 g dietary fiber; 33 g protein.

Easy Meatball Stroganoff

If you want to eat something uncommon and a bit artsy with your cooking, why not try meatball stroganoff. When making this recipe, make sure the meatball is fully cooked before you combine with cream and noodles.

Servings: 4

Ingredients

1 tablespoon **olive oil**

3 cups uncooked **egg noodles**

1 package (12 ounces) thawed **Italian meatballs**

1-1/2 cups **beef broth**

3/4 teaspoon dried **basil**

1 teaspoon dried **parsley flakes**

1/2 teaspoon **salt**

1/2 teaspoon **dried oregano**

3/4 cup **sour cream**

1/4 teaspoon **pepper**

1 cup **heavy whipping cream**

Directions

Follow the package directions when cooking the egg noodles and drain.

In a large skillet with heated oil on medium-high heat, brown the meatballs and remove from the pan, set aside.

Pour the broth to the skillet to detach the brown bits from the sides. Stir in seasonings and bring mixture to a boil. Cook for five to seven minutes until the liquid has reduced to half a cup.

Pour the cream, cooked noodles and browned meatballs to the broth, stir and boil.

Simmer on low heat with cover for three to five minutes until a bit thickened.

Add sour cream, stir and heat thoroughly.

Serve!

Nutritional Information: 717 calories; 172 mg cholesterol; 57 g fat (30 g saturated fat); 31 g carbohydrate; 1291 mg sodium; 5 g total sugars; 2 g dietary fiber; 20 g protein.

Saucy Skillet Lasagna

This hearty lasagna is quick to do since you do not need to cool the noodles and drain. This no-cook lasagna recipe is cheesy and saucy that will surely be a favorite comfort food in your home. You can use ground pork or chicken if you wish instead of beef for a twist.

Servings: 8

Ingredients

1 package (9 ounces) **no-cook lasagna noodles**

1 pound **ground beef**

1 can (14-1/2 ounces) undrained diced **tomatoes**

2 lightly beaten large **eggs**

1-1/2 cups **ricotta cheese**

4 cups **marinara sauce**

Optional:

1 cup shredded **part-skim mozzarella cheese**

Directions

Cook on moderate heat the ground beef in a large skillet for six to eight minutes until the color is no longer pink. Break beef into crumbles and drain.

Transfer beef to a large bowl and stir in tomatoes.

Combine ricotta cheese and eggs in a small bowl.

Evenly spread one cup of meat mixture in the skillet.

Lay one cup ricotta mixture, and pour 1 ½ cups marinara sauce and followed by half of the lasagna noodles, and break the noodles to fit in if needed.

Repeat the same steps and finally, spread the remainder of marinara sauce on top.

Bring the lasagna mixture to a boil and simmer with cover for fifteen to seventeen minutes until the lasagna noodles are tender. Remove skillet from heat.

Sprinkle on top with mozzarella cheese and let it melt for two seconds.

Enjoy!

Nutritional Information: 430 calories; 108 mg cholesterol; 18 g fat (8 g saturated fat); 750 mg sodium; 41 g carbohydrate; 11 g total sugars; 4 g dietary fiber; 27 g protein.

RAVIOLI WITH SNAP PEAS & MUSHROOMS

This quickie pasta recipe is a time-saver and it helps remove your worries whenever the kids ask for something to eat. It's 100% sure that your kiddos will love the crunchy texture and creamy taste of this dish.

Servings: 8

Ingredients

1 pound trimmed fresh **sugar snap peas**

1 package (20 ounces) cold **cheese ravioli**

1 tablespoon **butter**

1/2 pound sliced fresh **mushrooms**

3 finely chopped **shallots**

2 minced **garlic cloves**

2 cups **fat-free evaporated milk**

1 teaspoon grated **lemon peel**

1 teaspoon **lemon-pepper seasoning**

8 thinly sliced fresh **sage leaves**

1/4 teaspoon **white pepper**

1/4 cup shredded **Parmesan cheese**

1/4 cup **hazelnuts**

Note: If sage leaves are not available, replace it with 2 teaspoons of rubbed sage.

Directions

Coarsely chop the nuts and toast by baking in a shallow pan at 350 degrees F for five to ten minutes or by cooking in a skillet on low heat and stir until lightly browned.

Cook ravioli in a large saucepan, al dente. Add the snap beans three minutes before the last cooking time and drain.

Heat the butter in a large skillet on moderate high heat.

Stir fry the mushrooms, garlic and shallots, cooking and stirring until the mushrooms are tender.

Add milk, lemon peel, white pepper, and sage, and bring to a boil.

Remove cover and simmer on low heat for two minutes until the sauce is a bit thickened.

Place the snap peas and ravioli to the sauce, stir to incorporate.

Sprinkle pasta with parmesan cheese and toasted hazelnuts.

Serve!

Nutritional Information: 347 calories; 36 mg cholesterol; 11 g fat (5 g saturated fat); 44 g carbohydrate; 470 mg sodium; 11 g total sugars; 4 g dietary fiber); 20 g protein.

LEMONY SHRIMP & SNOW PEA PASTA

This pasta is a healthy option if you are avoiding meat. The lemon dressing is added to the shrimp mixture before coating the pasta. You can use mixed herbs for garnish, and for pasta, you can choose corkscrews or bow ties.

Servings: 6

Ingredients

1 3/4 cups uncooked **spiral pasta** or **gemelli**

2 tablespoons **olive oil**, divided

1 pound uncooked **shrimp** (26-30 per pound)

2 cups fresh **snow peas**

3 minced **garlic cloves**

3/4 teaspoon **salt**, divided

1/4 teaspoon plus 1/8 teaspoon **pepper**, divided

1 cup **grape tomatoes**, halved

Dressing:

2 tablespoons **fresh parsley**, chopped

1/4 cup **lemon juice**

2 tablespoons **olive oil**

2 minced **garlic cloves**

2 teaspoons grated **lemon zest**

Garnish:

Additional grated **lemon zest**

Chopped **fresh parsley**

Directions

Peel and devein uncooked shrimp, set aside.

Cook the pasta by following the package directions, drain and reserve ½ of the liquid for later use.

Heat one tablespoon of oil in a large nonstick pan on moderate heat.

Sauté the peas, stir and cook for two to three minutes until crisp and tender. Remove and transfer in a bowl.

Heat the remaining oil in the same pan to moderate-high heat.

Sauté the shrimp, stir and cook for two to three minutes until pinkish.

Stir fry garlic and add ¼ teaspoon pepper, and ½ teaspoon salt; cook for another 1 minute.

In same pan, heat remaining oil over medium-high heat. Add shrimp; cook and stir 2-3 minutes or until shrimp turns pink.

Add garlic, 1/2 teaspoon salt and 1/4 teaspoon pepper; cook and stir 1 minute longer.

Add the cooked pasta to the shrimp mixture together with the tomatoes and peas, toss to blend well.

Whisk in a small bowl the lemon juice, oil, parsley, lemon zest, garlic and the remaining pepper and salt until incorporated and pour over the shrimp mixture.

Toss to coat well and add the pasta liquid to moisten the mixture.

Garnish with parsley and lemon zest.

Enjoy!

Nutritional Information: 279 calories; 92 mg cholesterol; 11 g fat (2 g saturated fat); 28 g carbohydrate; 390 mg sodium; 3 g sugars; 2 g dietary fiber; 18 g protein.

Vegetarian Linguine

This pasta dish is so easy to prepare by combining the cooked linguine and the sautéed vegetables. If you are avoiding meat, this is your healthy alternative too. Its taste is so cheesy and the texture is crisp-tender.

Servings: 6

Ingredients

2 tablespoons **butter**

6 ounces **uncooked linguine**

1 tablespoon **olive oil**

2 medium thinly sliced **zucchini**

1/2 pound sliced fresh **mushrooms**

1 large chopped **tomato**

1/4 teaspoon **pepper**

2 chopped **green onions**

1 minced **garlic clove**

1/2 teaspoon **salt**

3 tablespoons shredded **Parmesan cheese**

1 cup shredded **provolone cheese**

2 teaspoons minced fresh **basil**

Directions

Follow the package direction in cooking the linguine, drain and set aside.

Heat in a large skillet the butter and oil combined on medium heat.

Sauté the mushrooms and zucchini and cook for three to five minutes.

Stir fry the tomato, garlic, onions and the seasonings. Simmer with cover on low heat for three minutes.

Add the vegetable mixture to the linguine.

Toss to coat and sprinkle with basil and cheeses. Toss again to combine well.

Enjoy!

Nutritional Information: 260 calories; 25 mg cholesterol; 13 g fat (7 g saturated fat); 26 g carbohydrate; 444 mg sodium; 3 g total sugars; 2 g dietary fiber; 12 g protein.

Blushing Penne Pasta

What happens when wine is incorporated with spices in a dish? The answer is a rich, creamy and flavorful dish, like this Blushing Penne Pasta. You can use vodka if white wine is unavailable and whipping cream instead of half-and-half.

Servings: 8

Ingredients

2 tablespoons **butter**

1 package (16 ounces) **penne pasta**

2 tablespoons minced fresh **basil**

1 medium **onion** (cut into half and thinly sliced)

2 tablespoons minced fresh **thyme**

1 teaspoon **salt**

1-1/2 cups **half-and-half cream**, divided

1/2 cup **white wine**

2 tablespoons **all-purpose flour**

1 tablespoon **tomato paste**

1/2 cup shredded **Parmigiano-Reggiano cheese** (divided)

Note: Two tablespoons fresh thyme can be replaced with two teaspoons of dried thyme. Two tablespoons fresh basil can be replaced with 2 teaspoons dried basil. White wine can be replaced with reduced-sodium chicken broth.

Directions

Cook pasta in a six-quart stockpot al dente; drain and return to the pot.

Heat the butter in a large pan and sauté the onion over moderate heat for eight to ten minutes until aromatic.

Stir fry the herbs and season with salt; stir and cook for 1 minute.

Pour the wine, 1 cup cream and tomato paste, stirring often to incorporate.

Combine the remainder of the cream and the flour, stir until smooth.

Slowly add the flour mixture into the onion mixture; bring to a boil, stirring frequently for two minutes, until thickened.

Add one-fourth cup cheese and stir into pasta. Sprinkle remaining cheese on top.

Enjoy!

Nutritional Information: 335 calories; 34 mg cholesterol; 10 g fat (6 g saturated fat); 47 g carbohydrate; 431 mg sodium; 4 g total sugars; 2 g dietary fiber; 12 g protein.

Italian Sausage with Artichokes and Feta

This hearty masterpiece will wow your guests. It has the best taste in so far as pasta dishes are concerned. It uses gemelli pasta and blend with Italian sausage, artichoke hearts and feta cheese.

Servings: 4

Ingredients

Hot cooked **gemelli pasta** or **spiral pasta**

1 pound **Italian sausage**

1minced **garlic clove**

1 finely chopped small **red onion**

1 jar (7-1/2 ounces) **marinated quartered artichoke hearts**

1/4 cup **dry red wine** or **chicken broth**

1/2 cup **tomato sauce**

1/2 teaspoon **Italian seasoning**

1/2 cup crumbled **feta cheese**

Minced fresh **parsley** (optional)

Directions

Drain artichoke hearts and chop coarsely, set aside.

Cook the sausage in a large skillet together with the garlic and onion over moderate heat for six to eight minutes, breaking up the sausage to crumble. Drain cooked sausage, set aside.

Stir in tomato sauce, artichoke hearts, Italian seasoning and wine until thoroughly heated.

Slowly stir in cheese and sprinkle with parsley if necessary. Serve sauce with pasta.

Note: Frozen sausage should be thawed in the refrigerator overnight when ready to use by the following day.

Serve!

Nutritional Information: 435 calories; 69 mg cholesterol; 9 g carbohydrate; 35 g fat (11 g saturated fat); 1149 mg sodium; 5 g total sugars; 1 g dietary fiber; 16 g protein.

Turkey Picadillo

This quickie pasta recipe won't make you sweat. Make sure the turkey is cooked thoroughly, and the sauce will be served with the cooked pasta. The top of the pasta is garnished with the sour cream and green onions.

Servings: 4

Ingredients

1 pound **lean ground turkey**

5 1/3 cups uncooked **whole wheat egg noodles**

1 medium chopped **green pepper**

1 chopped small **onion**

2 minced **garlic cloves**

2 teaspoons **chili powder**

2 **minced garlic cloves**

1/4 teaspoon **pepper**

1 can (14-1/2 ounces) undrained **Italian diced tomatoes**

1/2 cup **golden raisins**

Reduced-fat sour cream

Optional:

Chopped **green onions**

Directions

Follow the package directions when preparing the noodles, drain and return to pot.

In a large nonstick pan, cook the turkey, onion and green pepper on moderate heat until pink color is gone. Drain the turkey.

In the same pan, stir the garlic, pepper and chili powder and cook for one more minute.

Stir in raisins and tomatoes and heat thoroughly.

Serve noodles with the turkey mixture. Drizzle with sour cream and sprinkle with green onions.

Serve!

Nutritional Information: 463 calories; 90 mg cholesterol; 11 g fat (3 g saturated fat); 69 g carbohydrate; 535 mg sodium; 19 g total sugars; 9 g dietary fiber; 30 g protein.

PEANUT GINGER PASTA

Peanut lovers must be very happy with this flavorful and aromatic pasta, which is a fusion of lime juice, lime zest, basil, ginger and your favorite peanut butter. This Peanut Ginger Pasta is a bit soothing to the throat and luscious to eat. This is a sample of how Thai cuisine tastes like.

Servings: 4

Ingredients

8 ounces uncooked **whole wheat linguine**

1/4 cup **lime juice**

2 tablespoons **reduced-sodium soy sauce**

2 1/2 teaspoons grated **lime zest**

2 teaspoons **water**

1 teaspoon **sesame oil**

1/3 cup **creamy peanut butter**

2-1/2 teaspoons minced fresh **gingerroot**

2 minced **garlic cloves**, minced

1/4 teaspoon **salt**

1/4 teaspoon **pepper**

2 cups small fresh **broccoli florets**

2 medium **carrots**, grated

1 medium julienned **sweet red pepper**

2 chopped **green onions**

2 tablespoons fresh **basil**, minced

Directions

Place the lime zest, lime juice, soy sauce, water, sesame oil, peanut butter, gingerroot, garlic cloves and salt in a food processor; cover and blend until incorporated.

Cook the pasta by following the direction on the package.

Add broccoli to the pasta while five minutes are left for cooking time.

Drain together and transfer to a large mixing bowl.

Add the carrots, pepper, onions and basil, and toss.

Add the peanut butter to the mixture and toss to coat.

Enjoy!

Nutritional Information: 365 calories; 0 cholesterol; 13 g fat (2 g saturated fat); 567 mg sodium; 57 g carbohydrate; 6 g total sugars; 10 g fiber; 14 g protein.

Asparagus Ham Dinner

This easy Asparagus Dinner Ham will make your day great as it is loaded with nutrients from the fresh asparagus, tomatoes, pepper, and parsley. The pasta is added to the vegetables and topped with cheese.

Servings: 6

Ingredients

2 cups uncooked **corkscrew (spiral pasta)**

1 tablespoon **olive oil**

3/4 pound fresh **asparagus**

1 julienned medium **sweet yellow pepper**

6 diced medium **tomatoes**

6 ounces cubed boneless fully cooked **ham**

1/2 teaspoon dried **oregano**

1/4 cup minced fresh **parsley**

1/2 teaspoon **salt**

1/2 teaspoon **dried basil**

1/4 cup shredded **Parmesan cheese**

1/8 to 1/4 teaspoon **cayenne pepper**

Directions

Cut asparagus into one-inch pieces, set aside.

Cook pasta by following what is directed in the package; drain set aside.

Sauté yellow pepper and asparagus in hot oil of your large cast-iron. Cook and stir until crisp-gender.

Sauté the ham and tomatoes until thoroughly heated. Add drained pasta to the vegetable mixture, stir.

Add parsley and seasonings, stir until coated. Top with cheese before serving.

Enjoy!

Nutritional Information: 204 calories; 17 mg cholesterol; 5 g fat (1 g saturated fat); 561 mg sodium; 29 g carbohydrate; 5 g total sugars; 3 g dietary fiber; 12 g protein.

Creamy Sausage-Mushroom Rigatoni

Love the taste of mushrooms and sausage in a creamy and peppery mixture. It cinches to give you a taste of Italy with this luscious rigatoni recipe very quickly. You don't have to go to Italia to savor pasta dishes because you can always have them prepare in your home, like this recipe.

Servings: 6

Ingredients

1 pound **Italian sausage**

1 package (16 ounces) **rigatoni**

2 teaspoons **butter**

2 minced **garlic cloves**

1 pound sliced **fresh mushrooms**

1/2 teaspoon **salt**

2 cups **heavy whipping cream**

1/4 teaspoon **pepper**

Optional:

Minced fresh **parsley**

Directions

In a six-quart cooking pot, cook the rigatoni according to package directions. Drain and return to the pot.

Cook the sausage in a large pan on moderate heat for four to six minutes until the pinkish color is not visible. Stir often and break into crumbles and drain. Remove the sausage from pan, set aside.

Heat the butter on moderate heat in the same pan.

Stir fry the garlic, mushrooms, pepper and salt. Cover, stir often and cook for four minutes.

Remove the cover and continue stirring for two to three minutes until the liquid is reduced and the mushrooms are tender. Add cream and lightly bring to a boil.

Simmer on low heat and continue cooking uncovered for eight to ten minutes until the mixture is consistent.

Heat the sausage thoroughly in the pan.

Serve pasta with the sauce and garnish with parsley if desired.

Serve!

Nutritional Information: 570 calories; 115 mg cholesterol; 37 g fat (19 g saturated fat); 529 mg sodium; 46 g carbohydrate; 5 g total sugars; 3 g dietary fiber; 17 g protein.

Jiffy Ground Pork Skillet

Meat lovers must rejoice with this mouthwatering pasta dish. The meaty, saucy and flavorful pasta mixture is tossed with the penne pasta and zucchini to make every bite enjoyable and satisfying.

Servings: 5

Ingredients

1 pound **ground pork**

1/2 cup chopped **onion**

1 1/2 cups uncooked **penne pasta**

1 can (14-1/2 ounces) undrained **stewed tomatoes**

1 teaspoon **Italian seasoning**

1 can (8 ounces) **tomato sauce**

1 medium **zucchini**

Directions

Cut zucchini into one-fourth inch slices, set aside.

Place pasta in a pot and cook according to package directions; drain and set aside.

Cook the onion and pork in a large pan on moderate heat until the meat is not pinkish anymore, and drain.

Add the Italian seasonings, tomato sauce and tomatoes to the meat and bring to a boil.

Simmer with cover and cook until all flavors are incorporated for five minutes.

Add the cooked pasta to the skillet, add the zucchini and stir.

Cover the mixture and cook for three to five minutes until the vegetable is crisp-tender.

Note: If preparing a make ahead, transfer portions of the cooled pasta mixture in a Ziplock bag for later use. When ready to use, thaw in the refrigerator for several hours. Reheat thawed pasta mixture in a saucepan, stir often and add a little amount of tomato sauce if desired.

Serve!

Nutritional Information: 317 calories; 61 mg cholesterol; 14 g fat (5 g saturated fat); 27 g carbohydrate; 408 mg sodium; 7 g total sugars; 2 g dietary fiber; 21 g protein.

Beef & Spinach Lo Mein

Stir fried vegetables and meat and added to the spaghetti will make your meal heavy, so you don't have to look for another dish. This crunchy, meaty and saucy dish will make your loved ones ask for a second helping.

Servings: 5

Ingredients

2 tablespoons **soy sauce**

1/4 cup **hoisin sauce**

2 teaspoons **sesame oil**

1 tablespoon **water**

2 minced **garlic cloves**

1/4 teaspoon **red pepper flakes**, crushed

1 pound thinly sliced **beef top round steak**

6 ounces uncooked **spaghetti**

4 teaspoons **canola oil**, divided

1 can (8 ounces) drained sliced **water chestnuts**

2 sliced **green onions**

1 package (10 ounces) coarsely chopped fresh **spinach**

1 seeded and thinly sliced **red chili pepper**

Directions

Cook the spaghetti according to what is instructed in the package, drain.

Combine in a small bowl the hoisin sauce, soy sauce, water, sesame oil, garlic cloves and red pepper flakes.

Remove one-fourth cup of the mixture and transfer to a large bowl; stir in beef and toss to combine well, marinate for ten minutes at room temperature.

Heat the 1 ½ teaspoons of canola oil in a skillet. Stir fry one-half of the beef mixture for one to two minutes until no longer pinkish. Remove beef from pan.

Pour another same amount of oil and cook the remaining of the beef mixture.

Sauté the green onions and water chestnuts in the remaining oil for thirty seconds.

Add spinach and last batch of hoisin mixture until the vegetable is wilted.

Pour the beef to the pan and heat thoroughly. Add the drained spaghetti to the beef mixture and toss to incorporate.

Garnish with chili pepper.

Serve!

Nutritional Information: 363 calories; 51 mg cholesterol; 10 g fat (2 g saturated fat); 40 g carbohydrate; 652 mg sodium; 6 g total sugars; 4 g dietary fiber; 28 g protein.

WEEKNIGHT PASTA SQUIGGLES

This pasta dish is something that you will always look forward because of its cheesy taste and zesty flavor. It does not require a long list of ingredients and steps, an ideal recipe for busy people.

Servings: 8

Ingredients

1 can (28 ounces) **whole plum tomatoes with basil**

1 package (19.5 ounces) **Italian turkey sausage links**

1 can (14.5 ounces) **no-salt-added whole tomatoes**

4 cups **uncooked spiral pasta**

1 can (14.5 ounces) **reduced-sodium chicken broth**

1/4 cup **water**

1/2 cup crumbled **goat cheese or feta cheese**.

Directions

Remove casings of the sausage links, set aside.

Coarsely chop the tomatoes and reserve the juice, set aside.

Place in a Dutch oven the sausage; cook for five to seven minutes, and crumble on moderate high heat until pinkish color is gone.

Pour the reserved tomato juice and the tomatoes, stir to combine.

Add pasta, water and chicken broth, bring to a boil. Simmer on medium heat with cover until the pasta is cooked al dente for fifteen to eighteen minutes. Stir often and top with cheese.

Enjoy!

Nutritional Information: 278 calories; 34 mg cholesterol; 7g fat (2g saturated fat); 622mg sodium;38g carbohydrate;5 g total sugars; 4 g dietary fiber; 16 g protein.

Steak & Mushroom Stroganoff

This versatile recipe can be served for your family dinner and for special occasions. Its creamy sauce makes every bite more exciting. The sauce is a mixture of butter, beef broth, fresh mushrooms, shallots and sour cream

Servings: 6

Ingredients

1 ½ pounds **beef top sirloin steak**

6 cups **uncooked egg noodles**

1/2 teaspoon **salt**

1 tablespoon **canola oil**

1/2 teaspoon **pepper**

1/2 cup **beef broth**

2 tablespoons **butter**

1 pound sliced fresh **mushrooms**

1 tablespoon **fresh dill**, snipped

2 finely chopped **shallots**

1 cup **sour cream**

Directions

Cut sirloin steak into 2x1/2-inch strips, set aside.

Follow the noodle's package direction when cooking and drain.

Toss the steak with salt, pepper and oil. Heat on moderate heat a large pan and sauté half of the steak for two to three minutes until browned.

Remove beef from pan and cook the remaining beef.

Heat the butter on moderate high heat in the same pan.

Sauté the mushrooms for four to six minutes until browned lightly.

Stir fry the shallots, cook for one to two minutes until tender.

Pour the beef broth, beef and dill, stir until thoroughly heated. Simmer on medium heat.

Pour the sour cream and stir until combined well. Serve with cooked noodles.

Serve!

Nutritional Information: 455 calories; 115 mg cholesterol; 19 g fat (10 g saturated fat); 379 mg sodium; 34 g carbohydrate; 4 g total sugars; 2 g dietary fiber; 34 g protein.

Barbecue Pork and Penne Skillet

Quick meals like this recipe, is an easy way to feed your entire family, without really trying hard. With a quick glance of the recipe, for sure you will know how to prepare this peppery, creamy and saucy pasta dish.

Servings: 8

Ingredients

1 package (16 ounces) **penne pasta**

3/4 cup chopped **onion**

3 minced **garlic cloves**

1 cup chopped **sweet red pepper**

1 tablespoon **butter**

1 tablespoon **olive oil**

1 can (14-1/2 ounces) diced undrained **tomatoes with mild green chilies**

1/2 cup **beef broth**

1 teaspoon **ground cumin**

1 box (16 ounces) **fully cooked barbecued shredded pork** (chilled)

1 teaspoon **pepper**

1/4 teaspoon **salt**

1-1/4 cups shredded **cheddar cheese**

1/4 cup chopped **green onions**

Directions

Cook the pasta al dente, drain and set aside.

Heat the oil and butter in a large skillet and sauté the onion and red pepper until tender.

Sauté and stir the garlic for one minute. Add the pork, beef broth, tomatoes, pepper, salt and cumin; stir until thoroughly heated.

Add the cheese and pasta to the pork-spices mixture; stir to combine.

Sprinkle on top with minced green onions.

Note: Make ahead by freezing the cooled pasta mixture in Ziploc bag. Thaw the night before and place in a heat-proof dish; microwave on high until heated thoroughly.

Enjoy!

Nutritional Information: 428 calories; 40 mg cholesterol; 11 g fat (6 g saturated fat); 903 mg sodium; 61 g carbohydrate; 16 g sugars; 4 g dietary fiber; 20 g protein.

Italian Sausage with Bow Ties

Serve this luscious crumbled Italian sausage mixed with pasta. The peppery-cheesy sauce is a blend of tomatoes, spices, cream and cheese, stir fried and seasoned. You will always crave for this dish as it has a pleasant and tempting taste.

Servings: 6

Ingredients

1 pound **Italian sausage**

1 package (16 ounces) **bow tie pasta**

1/2 cup chopped **onion**

2 cans (14 ½ oz. each) drained and chopped **Italian stewed tomatoes**

1/2 teaspoon crushed **red pepper flakes**

1-1/2 teaspoons minced **garlic**

1 1/2 cups **heavy whipping cream**

1/4 teaspoon dried **basil**

1/4 teaspoon **salt**

1/4 teaspoon dried **basil**

Shredded **Parmesan cheese**

Directions

Cook the pasta in a pot and follow the package instructions; drain and set aside.

Cook in a six-quart stockpot the sausage and crumble with the pepper flakes and onion over moderate heat.

Stir and cook for 5 to 7 minutes until pinkish color has disappeared.

Stir fry garlic for one minute and drain.

Stir fry tomatoes, salt, basil and cream and bring to a boil on moderate heat.

Simmer on low heat without a cover for six to eight minutes until consistent; stir often to blend.

Add the cooked pasta, stir until heated thoroughly. Serve pasta with cheese.

Enjoy!

Nutritional Information: 751 calories; 119 mg cholesterol; 44 g fat (21 g saturated fat); 989 mg sodium; 67 g carbohydrate; 9 g total sugars; 4 g dietary fiber; 23 g protein.

Chorizo Pumpkin Pasta

This hot and spicy pasta provides an answer to your cravings. Chorizo Pumpkin Pasta is ideal for you, no matter what time you arrive at night, you can quickly prepare this recipe. You can store the pasta mixture in the freezer for a week, so when you come home late, you have something to eat.

Servings: 6

Ingredients

3 cups **gemelli** *or* **spiral pasta** (uncooked)

1 package (12 ounces) fully cooked **chorizo chicken sausage links**

1 cup canned **pumpkin**

1 cup **half-and-half cream**

3/4 teaspoon **salt**

1/4 teaspoon **pepper**

3/4 teaspoon salt

1 1/2 cups shredded **Manchego cheese**

Optional:

Minced fresh **cilantro**

Note: Try Monterey Jack cheese if Manchego is not available.

Directions

Cook the pasta in a deep stockpot with water and follow the package instructions, drain and reserve three-fourth cup of pasta liquid. Set aside.

Sauté the sausage in a large pan on medium heat until a bit browned. Simmer on medium-low heat.

Stir fry the pumpkin, half-and-half cream, pepper and salt. Cook and continue stirring until heated thoroughly.

Add the mixture to the pasta and reserved liquid to moisten. Toss to combine and stir in cheese.

Garnish pasta with cilantro.

Enjoy!

Nutritional Information: 471 calories; 92 mg cholesterol; 20 g fat (11 g saturated fat); 847 mg sodium; 48 g carbohydrate; 7 g total sugars; 3 g dietary fiber; 26 g protein.

BUCATINI WITH SAUSAGE & KALE

Bucatini pasta is combined with the spicy Italian sausage, fresh kale and spices for a romantic evening with your sweetheart. You can also use fettuccine instead of bucatini. The taste is just the same: yummy and hot.

Servings: 6

Ingredients

1 package (12 ounces) **bucatini pasta** or **fettuccine**

1 pound spicy or regular **Johnsonville Ground Mild Italian sausage**

2 teaspoons **olive oil**

Additional 3 tablespoons **olive oil**

5 thinly sliced **garlic cloves**

3/4 teaspoon **salt**

8 cups chopped fresh **kale**

1/4 teaspoon **pepper**

Shredded **Romano cheese**

Directions

Cook the pasta in a large pot and follow what is instructed in the package. Drain and reserve two cups of the pasta liquid. Pour two teaspoons of oil and toss. Set aside.

Cook sausage in a six-quart stockpot on moderate heat for five to seven minutes until pink color has disappeared.

Break sausage into larger crumbles, stir often.

Pour 3 tablespoons of oil and sauté the garlic for two minutes.

Stir fry the kale, pepper and salt; cook on moderate heat for ten minutes until tender, stir frequently.

Add the pasta and the reserved liquid and boil. Simmer without cover on low heat until the pasta is al dente and the liquid has reduced, for three minutes. Toss to combine.

Sprinkle on top with cheese.

Enjoy!

Nutritional Information: 512 calories; 51mg cholesterol; 30 g fat (8 g saturated fat); 898 mg sodium; 43g carbohydrate; 2 g total sugars; 3 g dietary fiber; 19 g protein.

Ravioli with Apple Chicken Sausage

There is so much excitement in preparing this vegetable-chicken pasta. This is because it can be done in haste. Just imagine how fast you can prepare this recipe and in no time, you have your creamy, sweet and saucy pasta to your table.

Servings: 4

Ingredients

1 package (12 oz.) fully cooked **apple chicken sausage links slices**

1 package (18 oz.) frozen **butternut squash ravioli**

2 packages (10 oz. each) frozen **creamed spinach**

1 tablespoon **olive oil**

1 teaspoon **maple syrup**

1/4 teaspoon **pumpkin pie spice**

Directions

Cut sausage into one-half inch slices, set aside.

Cook ravioli based on package directions, drain.

Prepare the spinach as per package instructions. Heat the oil in a large skillet on medium heat.

Stir fry the sausage for 2 to 4 minutes until brown.

Add the cooked ravioli, maple syrup, spinach and pie spice to the sausage. Stir to combine well and thoroughly heated.

Enjoy!

Nutritional Information: 622 calories; 64 mg cholesterol; 20 g fat (6 g saturated fat); 2098 mg sodium; 81 g carbohydrate: 25 g total sugars; 6 g dietary fiber; 30 g protein.

Thai Lime Shrimp & Noodles

Have a taste of authentic Thai lime shrimp added to your pasta. It tastes chilly hot and creamy due to the right blend of Thai red chili paste, gingerroot, coconut milk and spices. This union of Asian and Italian dish is enough to make your stomach full.

Servings: 6

Ingredients

3 tablespoons **lime juice**

4 teaspoons **Thai red chili paste**

1 cup minced fresh **basil**

1 minced **garlic clove**

1 ½ pounds uncooked **shrimp** (26-30 per pound)

1 teaspoon minced fresh **gingerroot**

12 ounces uncooked **angel hair pasta**

4 **teaspoons olive oil**, divided

1 can (14 ½ oz.) **chicken broth**

1 can (13.66 Oz.) **coconut milk**

2 tablespoons grated **lime zest**

2 tablespoons of **cold water**

1 teaspoon **salt**

1 tablespoon **cornstarch**

Directions

Cook the pasta al dente, drain and set aside.

Peel and devein the shrimp, set aside.

Place in a blender the, lime juice, basil, chili paste, garlic clove, and the gingerroot, cover and blend. Spoon one tablespoon of mixture and mix with the shrimp.

Heat two teaspoons of oil in a large pan on medium high heat.

Pour half of the shrimp mixture and stir fry for two to four minutes until pinkish. Remove shrimp from the pan and keep warm.

Heat another two teaspoons of oil and pour the remainder of the shrimp and stir fry for two to four minutes until there is no pink color anymore.

Add the chicken broth, salt, coconut milk and the remainder of the basil mixture to the same pan.

Mix in a small bowl the water and cornstarch, stir until smooth, and add to the broth mixture.

Stir and boil, and cook for one to two minutes until thickened a bit. Add lime zest and stir. Add the pasta and the shrimp to the sauce. Toss to coat.

Serve!

Nutritional Information: 486 calories; 141 mg cholesterol; 20 g fat (13 g saturated fat); 865 mg sodium; 49 g carbohydrate; 3 g total sugars; 2 g dietary fiber; 28 g protein.

HAY AND STRAW

Aside from its unique name, this recipe is quick to prepare in a jiffy, no more ceremonies to do. Just cook the pasta, sauté the ingredients and toss. The taste, oh so, wonderful; it is creamy, buttery, and cheesy.

Servings: 8

Ingredients

2 cups fully cooke**d ham**, julienned

1 package (16 ounces) **linguine**

3 cups frozen **peas**

1 tablespoon **butter**

1/3 cup heavy **whipping cream**

1 1/2 cups shredded **Parmesan cheese**

Directions

Cook the linguine as directed on the package, drain.

Heat in a large pan, the butter and sauté the ham for three minutes.

Stir and add the peas until heated. Toss the linguine with the Parmesan cheese, whipping cream and the ham mixture.

Serve!

Nutritional Information: 410 calories; 47 mg cholesterol; 14 g fat (7 g saturated fat); 783 mg sodium; 50 g carbohydrate; 6 g total sugars; 4 g dietary fiber; 23 g protein.

SPANISH NOODLES & GROUND BEEF

Impress you loved ones with your cooking skills by preparing this easy to do recipe. They might not be aware how easy this recipe is, despite its gorgeous appearance. The bacon is the secret behind its crunchiness that goes well with the saucy and spicy taste of this kitchen delight.

Servings: 4

Ingredients

3 1/4 cups uncooked medium **egg noodles**

1 small chopped **green pepper**

1/3 cup chopped **onion**

1 pound **ground beef**

1 can (14.5 ounces) undrained diced **tomatoes**

1 1/2 cups of **water**

1/4 cup **chili sauce**

1/4 teaspoon **salt**

4 cooked and crumbled **bacon strips**

1/8 teaspoon **pepper**

Directions

Cook in a large pan the beef together with the onion and green pepper, on medium heat until pink color has disappeared for five to seven minutes. Drain to remove excess fat.

Add the tomatoes, noodles, water, salt, and pepper, and chili sauce, stir and let boil.

Simmer on low heat for 15 to twenty minutes until the noodles are al dente. Stir frequently.

Garnish pasta with bacon strips.

Enjoy!

Nutritional Information: 409 calories; 104 mg cholesterol; 18g fat (6g saturated fat); 756 mg sodium; 33g carbohydrate;8 g total sugars; 3 g dietary fiber; 28 g protein.

Southwestern Goulash

Macaroni with sautéed beef, tomatoes, tomato sauce, corn and spices is equal to super delicious goulash. It is easy to prepare and does not need special talent to create a delightful family dish.

Servings: 6

Ingredients

1 pound (90% lean) **ground beef**

1 cup uncooked **elbow macaroni**

1 chopped medium **onion**

1 can (8 oz.) **tomato sauce**

1 can (28 oz.) undrained diced **tomatoes**

1 can (4 oz.) chopped **green chilies**

2/3 cup frozen **corn**

1/2 teaspoon ground **cumin**

1/2 teaspoon **pepper**

1/4 teaspoon **salt**

1/4 cup fresh **cilantro**, minced

Directions

Cook the macaroni based on package instructions; drain and set aside.

Cook and crumble in a six-quart stockpot the ground beef and onion for six to eight minutes on medium heat.

Continue cooking until pink color has vanished; drain to remove excess oil.

Add the tomatoes, corn, tomato sauce, dry seasonings, and chilies and boil.

Simmer on low heat without a cover for five minutes until the flavors are incorporated.

Stir the mixture in cilantro and macaroni.

Enjoy!

Nutritional Information: 224 calories; 37mg cholesterol; 6g fat (2g saturated fat); 567mg sodium; 24g carbohydrate;7 g total sugars; 4 g dietary fiber; 19 g protein.

Chicken Sausage & Gnocchi Skillet

Chicken sausage blended with vegetables plus an array of seasonings makes this gnocchi recipe so irresistible. Although the recipe does not take long to prepare, it does not compromise its great taste. It is flavorful, cheesy and peppery.

Servings: 4

Ingredients

2 (3 oz. each) sliced fully cooked **Italian chicken sausage links**

1 package (16 oz.) **potato gnocchi**

1/2 pound sliced **baby portobello mushrooms**

1 tablespoon **butter**

1 tablespoon **olive oil**

1 finely chopped **medium onion**

1 pound fresh **asparagus**

2 minced **garlic cloves**

2 tablespoons **white wine** or **chicken broth**

2 ounces herbed fresh **goat cheese**

2 tablespoons minced **fresh basil** (2 teaspoons **dried basil**)

1/4 teaspoon **salt**

1 tablespoon **lemon juice**

1/8 teaspoon **pepper**

Grated **Parmesan cheese**

Directions

Trim asparagus and cut into one-half-inch pieces, set aside.

Cook gnocchi as per package directions. Drain in a colander and set aside.

Meanwhile, heat in a large skillet the oil and butter on medium-high heat.

Stir-fry the sausage, onion and mushrooms until the vegetables are crisp-tender and the sausage is browned.

Stir-fry the garlic and asparagus and cook for two to three minutes.

Pour the wine and boil, and continue cooking until the liquid is reduced.

Stir in goat cheese, lemon juice, basil, pepper and salt.

Add the gnocchi to the mixture and stir to coat. Sprinkle the pasta with parmesan cheese.

Enjoy!

Nutritional Information: 454 calories; 58 mg cholesterol; 15 g fat (6 g saturated fat); 995 mg sodium; 56 g carbohydrate; 11 g sugars; 5 g dietary fiber; 21 g protein.

ARTICHOKE CHICKEN PASTA

Weeknights will never be the same again with this colorful and ultra-delicious chicken pasta with artichoke, broccoli florets, mushrooms, tomatoes and artichoke. Your guests and loved ones will surely love its delectable taste.

Servings: 4

Ingredients

2 **teaspoons all-purpose flour**

6 ounces **uncooked fettuccine**

1/3 cup **dry white wine** or **chicken broth**

3 teaspoons **olive oil**, divided

1/4 cup **reduced-sodium chicken broth**

1 pound **boneless skinless chicken breasts**

1/2 cup fresh **broccoli florets**

1/2 cup sliced **fresh mushrooms**

1/2 cup halved **cherry tomatoes**

2 **garlic cloves**, minced

1/2 teaspoon **dried oregano**

1 can (14 oz.) drained, halved water-packed **artichoke hearts**

1/2 teaspoon **salt**

1 tablespoon minced fresh **parsley**

1 tablespoon shredded **Parmesan cheese**

Directions

Cut chicken into strips, set aside. Cook fettuccine al dente; drain and set aside.

Combine in a small bowl the wine, chicken broth and flour, stir until smooth.

Prepare a nonstick skillet by coating with cooking spray and heat two tablespoons of oil on medium heat.

Stir-fry the chicken for two minutes until the center is no longer pink. Remove the chicken from skillet.

Pour the remaining oil in the same skillet, and heat over medium-high heat.

Stir-fry broccoli and cook for two minutes.

Add the tomatoes, garlic and mushrooms and cook for two minutes.

Add the artichoke hearts, salt, flour mixture and oregano, stir until well blended, boil and cook for one to two minutes until the mixture is thick.

Add chicken, parsley and fettuccine to the mixture, stir until heated thoroughly. Sprinkle on top with Parmesan cheese.

Serve!

Nutritional Information: 378 calories; 64mg cholesterol; 8g fat (2g saturated fat); 668mg sodium; 41g carbohydrate;2 g total sugars; 2 g dietary fiber; 33 g protein.

CONGRATULATIONS!

YOU HAVE MADE IT TO THE END ! AS A TOKEN OF OUR APPRECIATION PLEASE CLICK ON THE BOOK BELOW AND ENTER YOUR EMAIL ADDRESS TO SUBSCRIBE TO OUR NEWSLETTER & CLAIM YOUR FREE COOKBOOK!

SAVOUR PRESS
CAST IRON
PRESS
SAVOUR PIE
COOKBOOK
Tasty and Delicious Recipes!
SAVOUR PRESS
baking book

Also, by the editors at Savour Press's kitchen

The Chili Cookbook

The Quiche Cookbook

Indian Instant Pot Cookbook

The Cajun and Creole Cookbook

The Grill Cookbook

The Burger Book

The Ultimate Appetizers Cookbook

The West African Cookbook

Korean Seoul Cookbook

The Cast Iron Cookbook

The Holiday Cookbook

The Baking Book

The Crepe Cookbook

Conclusion

Thank you so much for downloading this eBook. We at Savour Press hope this book has increased your knowledge and skills in cooking some delectable pasta recipes. This eBook contains a curated list of what we believe to be the 30 best pasta recipes which tackle a variety of flavors and tastes using different kinds of pasta noodles. All different categories of pasta are represented such as bucatini, angel hair, macaroni, spaghetti, fettuccine, gnocchi, penne, ravioli, and a lot more. During the creation of this cookbook, our team has decided to come up with recipes that are quick to prepare and easy method of cooking, and that all ingredients are common, and are always available in your favorite grocery and online stores. Our recipes are colorful, delectable, mouthwatering and healthy. You will notice that each recipe, whether it is a vegetarian or non-vegetarian is loaded with greens and spices that are important to stay healthy. Each recipe has its own nutritional information based on the number of servings. All you need in a cookbook is found right here in this book.

We hope you will enjoy cooking with these recipes.

Thanks again for your support.

Happy Cooking!

Manufactured by Amazon.ca
Bolton, ON

29789251R00059